*Exposures*
*Tripod Poems*

This is an autobiographical work.

Exposures: Tripod Poems, Copyright © 2019
Eve West Bessier. All rights reserved.

ISBN: 978-1-7338478-2-7 (trade paperback)

Published by Falcon West Books, First Edition, 2019

10 9 8 7 6 5 4 3 2 1

Printed in the United States of America.

Cover design: Eve West Bessier

Other Falcon West Books by Eve West Bessier

New Rain, a visionary novel   2015
Roots Music: Listening to Jazz   2019

# Exposures

## Tripod Poems

Eve West Bessier

*Falcon West Books*

Acknowledgments

I extend my gratitude to the editors of the journals and anthologies in which the following poems from this collection were first published.

"Cedar-Habitat-Sabbatical," and "Saunter-Cast-Headway," appeared in *Writing in a Woman's Voice*, edited by Beate Sigriddaughter, 2019.

"Pearl-Soft-Element," titled as "After Your Fatal Jump," appeared in *Breaking Sad: What to Say After Loss, What Not to Say, and When to Just Show Up*, an anthology edited by Shelly Fisher and Jennifer Jones, 2017.

"Pearl-Soft-Element," "Flip Side-Undersell-Pragmatism," and "West-Lackluster-Convert," appeared in *Sacramento Voices*, an anthology edited by Phillip Larrea, 2014.

For all who have come through
unbearable loss and opened
to renewal and joy

## Introduction

I call these *Tripod Poems* because they balance on three points of focus: three words randomly chosen from a dictionary (one at a time), which become the title of the poem, are contained within the poem, and through serendipity bring forth unexpected insight.

I also call these *Tripod Poems* because, like a tripod, each poem is a device to hold the camera steady in order to get a clear exposure.

Each exposure is a rendering of deeply personal experience, a brief philosophical treatise, a candid self-revelation. Combined they create four albums documenting a seven-year transformational journey through loss to renewal.

# Table of Contents

## Album One

*In Memory of Gregory*

| | |
|---|---|
| Pearl – Soft – Element | 3 |
| Equilibrium – Tide – Slate | 4 |
| Sojourn – Raptors – Bright | 6 |
| Silence – Long Shot – Terra Firma | 7 |
| Thunder – Casualty – Rectify | 8 |
| Stutter – Frostbite – Educe | 10 |
| Miniature – Speak – Expose | 12 |
| Rubato – Lure – Averse | 14 |
| Photograph – Search – Blindside | 16 |
| Shadowbox – Amend – Console | 18 |
| Goldfinch – Radiant – Depreciate | 20 |
| Longitude – Confide – Shard | 22 |
| Magnetic – Vision – Sequester | 23 |
| Metamorphosis – Attain – Jerkwater | 24 |
| Timbre – Harmonize – Persevere | 26 |

# Album Two

*Inner Transformations*

| | |
|---|---|
| Waiting – Detritus – Slack | 31 |
| Flip Side – Undersell – Pragmatism | 32 |
| Amplitude – Shoulder – Lark | 34 |
| Cedar – Habitat – Sabbatical | 36 |
| Saunter – Cast – Headway | 37 |
| Irrepressible – Fickle – Pull | 38 |
| Reverse – Crevice – Multifaceted | 40 |
| Oleander – Chimera – Performance | 42 |
| Raven – Frontispiece – Scrawl | 44 |
| Sitting – Mentor – Conscious | 46 |
| Excavate – Recumbent – Artifact | 47 |
| Swoon – Engineer – Matrilineal | 48 |
| Half-hearted – Gusto – Habit | 49 |
| Scripture – Tanager – Lifeboat | 50 |
| Halting – Dark Horse – Signify | 52 |

## Album Three

*The Nature of Change*

| | |
|---|---|
| Osprey – Sapphire – Canopy | 57 |
| Retake – Tender – Duet | 58 |
| Nimble – Frenetic – Trimming | 60 |
| Waterfall – Quartz – Slick | 61 |
| Tymbal – Externalism – Taffeta | 62 |
| Sensitize – Apothecary – Porous | 63 |
| Revisit – Monologue – Finesse | 64 |
| Sepia – Narrow – Homograph | 66 |
| Bumblebee – Skin – Flight | 68 |
| Precipitate – Chartreuse – Wallflower | 69 |
| Humpback – Rush – Ideal | 70 |
| Whalebone – Whitecap – Whacked Out | 73 |
| Favorite – Unbounded – Crushing | 74 |
| Layer – Stand – Rational | 75 |
| Rocketry – Diffraction – Kidnap | 76 |

# Album Four

*Southwest Renewal*

| | |
|---|---|
| Meltdown – Reckless – Harebrained | 81 |
| West – Lackluster – Convert | 82 |
| Hilltop – Supposed – Notice | 84 |
| Sandstone – Discontented – Southwest | 86 |
| Motherland – Flank – Pungent | 88 |
| Haphazard – Quota – Capitulate | 90 |
| Vocation – Hike – Arid | 92 |
| Naturalist – Saturate – Heliocentric | 94 |
| Granulate – Slough – Evidence | 95 |
| Scenery – Expansive – Well-being | 96 |
| Indian Summer – Fetish – Cliffhanger | 98 |
| Infiltrate – Beget – Upward | 100 |

| | |
|---|---|
| About the Author | 103 |

# Album One

*In Memory of Gregory*

11-23-58 to 9-27-12

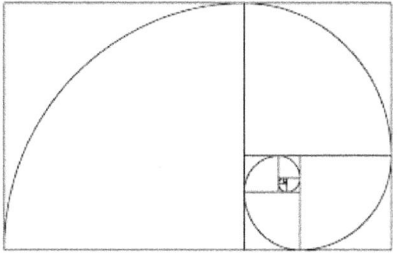

1, 1, 2, 3, 5, 8 ···

The Fibonacci Sequence
(also Gregory's birth date)

Pearl – Soft – Element

In the soft pumping
chambers of the heart,
an element of sorrow
can harden to resentment,
creating abrasive sediment.

Unlike the oyster,
wherein grit stimulates
layers of lustrous white
in the fertile dark
creating a pearl;

the heart that closes
on inconsolable loss
secretes no miraculous gloss
to coat the irritant
for radiant gain.

The heart can only create
its luminosity
by hurling clear
the calculus
of the unresolved,

exposing pain
to the ocean salt
of self-transparency.

Equilibrium – Tide – Slate

The man at the turn
of the tide
moves stones
placing each atop the other
as time grows into a life

moment by moment

Sometimes
all the stones fall
as scattered
Druid runes

and he begins again

methodically placing
the gray slate
into a balance
of weight
and shape

Even so
love shifts
and adjusts
to remain

to maintain

equilibrium

the falling too
a part of the balance

a way to rearrange

a gift of the wind

## Sojourn – Raptors – Bright

The solo fisherman with his hermetic heart
feels he is a part of the wilderness,
as an art of living, as a resonant frequency,
as a logarithmic equation of tender alchemy.

He sees the bald eagles seesaw in icy sky,
hears their piping cries above a frigid lake.
That sound, the only souvenir he will take.
That sound, and a spectrum-colored trout.

Then, sudden pain, accidental knife slice
deep into thumb, hot red drops on snow,
jolt of adrenaline, focused hike to the car,
an hour's drive to the nearest emergency room,

even then, the raptors sow him.

## Silence – Long Shot – Terra Firma

Sometimes a solitary act,
seemingly isolated,
arriving as arbitrary,
has the power to tear
the illusion of terra firma,
to radically alter
the course of a life.

Even if that act is one of kindness,
an intention aimed from the heart,
the alteration is not always kind.

I followed a love
that felt like home,

yet my life with you
only proved to amplify a loneliness
I did not feel so keenly before we met,

a deep deprivation so loud
it drowned out my happy inclinations,
until I became unable to silence
the shrieking absence of your affection.

Thunder – Casualty – Rectify

The gruff rumble of thunder
is innocuous, unless
it follows so tight on the heels
of lightning they coincide
in cataclysmic splendor.

Thunder sends the cat under the bed.
It sends me outside under the night sky
to observe the raging display
of electrical charges lacerate
a purple mantle of cloud-cover.

As the thunderclaps lapsed
less and less distant
from the instant
of retina-burning brilliance,

I should have known.
I should have taken cover.

I was dumbed-down by devotion,
a casualty of my belief in an ideal.

Now, I am struck
numb by the razor light
of the facts.

How do I rectify
a high voltage hit
to the heart?

## Stutter – Frostbite – Educe

mornings
I awaken
with emotional
frostbite

hard to thaw

even rudimentary
confidence,
seemingly irretrievable
after our dissolution

my incomprehensible
lack of astute
assessment
of your true
character

leaves me stupefied

I stumble
through

I stutter

until eventually
I begin
to complete
sentences

to relearn
the complex
mother tongue
of trusting

I will open
once more,
a morning glory,
an evening primrose

I will educe
myself

Miniature – Speak – Expose

Landfall of the revelation
that my perception
is at fault here

Everything flying
in the Category 5
tropical storm

over the sand
across the lawn
palm fronds
chaise lounges
even tree frogs

When I speak
only a hoarse croak,
the wind swallows
my voice

In the courtyard
a statue of Venus
a miniature
of the de Milo

wrenched from her pedestal
sucked up into the vortex
around the storm's eye

carried away

thrown harshly
into the roiling sea
without arms to swim

After the deluge
the silence is palpable

What I feared to expose

reared up
spat out
of the typhoon's
dragon mouth.

## Rubato – Lure – Averse

We stand at the edge of the wreckage
from the storm with the beautiful name

anesthetized by disbelief.

Sunlight reflects
off bent metal and wet cement.

Our neighborhood leveled
to a rubble so discordant
I find it impossible
to comprehend
we once lived here.

Only yesterday,
sipping morning coffee
at the cluttered kitchen counter,
placing roses in a blue vase.

Life's routines now so rubato
their melodies are indistinguishable
amid the sirens and silence.

I am not averse
to walking away,

without returning.

Yet, I am lured
into reminiscence
by evocative shards

a salt-water bloated photo album,

the puzzle of an unbroken porcelain plate,

a miniature brass whale breaching
from a sea of fractured blue glass,
blessed with rose petals.

Him I liberate.

Photograph – Search – Blindside

An image can blindside,
bring back time long tucked away
within the frames of photographs
at the bottom of the fancy scarf drawer
beneath things worn only occasionally.

I have very few images of you.
After the hard drive crash,
even the backup files were empty
of any evidence that we traveled
to Lake Alpine, San Diego, Desolation.

That first year, I hid everything
in dark places, wanting to erase
all traces that might unhinge me,
frantically hiding images, frames and all,
burying the betrayal of your smiling face.

Later, painfully taking you
completely out of the frames,
I place the images in a Ziplock bag
in a box on the top shelf
of the office closet.

So this unexpected image,
this tiny cameo, tucked
into a transparent pocket
sewn onto a small potpourri
heart-shaped pillow, meant to share
its light scent with garments,

this cameo of you by a glinting stream,
in your lizard T-shirt, gleam in your eyes,
still in love with me, still breathing,

this photograph that slipped
by my vigilant purge,
is a landmine I trigger
while I search for my perhaps
expired passport.

This image, itself a valid passport.

## Shadowbox – Amend – Console

I shadowbox a ghost.

Hard to know
if I've punched
a knockout blow,
or when to throw
in the towel.

Easier to feel
the percussive impact
of the jab to my jaw.
The Power Punch
to the breadbasket.
The left hook
to my right kidney.
The Sucker Punch
sending me down,
face first to kiss
the canvas.

I feel a deep need to amend

yet still defend
my entitlement
to console my soul
for inconsolable losses,

or to end this bout.
Just slip out
between the ropes.

Exit the ring,
still bewildered,
seeing stars
from the final
fatal Sunday Punch
to the temple

of Aphrodite.

## Goldfinch – Radiant – Depreciate

Watercolor
has small tolerance for error.

To fix mistakes is painstaking.

I paint the songbird,
its egg yolk yellow feathers,
its thin boned feet grasping
the blooming redbud branch.

Do I think for an instant
about how you always
found a way
to depreciate my art?

Do I call the goldfinch naïve or simplistic?

This cadmium bird is a radiant
contrast on a cerulean wash.

His bright eye stares into mine,
a triumph of surviving the long frost,
the dark season of incredulity.

Watercolor
allows reality to blur,
to run together,
become malleable

the way distanced
reflection
defies hard edges,

fixes mistakes
without remorse.

Longitude – Confide – Shard

What is the longitude of grief?

Where does the dateline fall
that moves us from dark to light?

What is the latitude of loss?

How might we confide
the broken shards
of our former selves
as secrets told,

travel them to more
temperate zones,

permit them
to be found out,

thawed out,

by our own
warming
kindness?

## Magnetic – Vision – Sequester

To describe a man
outside of his work, his craft, his art,
is to paint the mountain without its
rivers, clouds, rain, sunlight, birdsong.

To lay open the heart's treasures
is to perform a small miracle
in a crowded world, where noise
and movement dull and dampen,
while secrets sequester
beneath blanketed dreams.

I reach out through the trillion neutrinos
between us, spilling electrons in outer orbits,
pushing in opposition to magnetic tension

in order to achieve
a view of you.

Behold, the mountain in all its surrounds;
sound, vision, touch of light and air,
clearness of mind

there,
opens the heart
filling with wildflowers.

Metamorphosis – Attain – Jerkwater

My deck of cards depicts butterflies of the world.

You taught me to play this Solitaire,
building a pyramid of cards, brilliant wings
whittled down to attain a single card
remaining at the apex.

My favorite is the Blue Morpho,
for her bold elegance,
lapis lazuli, out-sized wings,
a gem of metamorphosis.

Today, a man came into the gallery
who looked like you might have looked
had you made it into your sixties.

Same straight Scottish nose,
high forehead, bald cranium.
Same stoic physical stance,
intelligent eyes, and warm,
arrestingly familiar handshake.

Dressed in a plaid flannel,
Black Watch tartan shirt,
jeans, baseball cap, he could
easily be your brother, even twin.

But both you and your brother
invited death in by your own will.

Still, this man is a woodworker,
just like you, an artist, a woodsman
moving to some jerkwater in Maine,
not afraid of a little cold, or a lot of it.

Just like you.

A random encounter,
like all the others here.

Yet, after nights of dreams
in which you appear,
speak to me, apologize
for being, *a total shit head*,
something you might have said,

after that,

I have to wonder.

## Timbre – Harmonize – Persevere

I miss the timbre of your voice.
Gentle, calm, welcoming.

You were a wood-whisperer,
coaxing a smooth finish,
conjoining elegant lines
to harmonize form and function.

I miss your warm hello
though not the authoritative tone
you took to condone
your own rational rightness
in the face of my instincts.

Today is Valentine's Day, again.
The only art you left me
is this collection of faded cards.

Each handmade, each unique,
filled with loving words
addressed to *My Genevieve*,
your term of endearment.

Hearts with gold overlay.
Hearts in white filigree.
Hearts cut out carefully
from red construction paper.

My heart cut out
so carelessly
by your words and deeds
it still leaves me reeling,
raging uselessly against
an immutable past tense.

Today, I persevere,
alone, hoping to coax
your lost voice
into a heart-shaped
music box.

# Album Two

*Inner Transformations*

Waiting – Detritus – Slack

I am still,
waiting

for the frenzied
centrifuge
inside my mind

to slack off

sending out its final halo
of spun out detritus

like the translucent spray
off a wet dog
shaking river wildness
into afternoon haze

I am still,
waiting

Flip Side – Undersell – Pragmatism

Once I sported
a magnificent
faith

A bravado of optimism
so keen
it radiated
a high beam,
illuminated the road ahead

That was before
the accidents of fate:
near fatal collisions
poorly executed merges
unattended yield signs
flat tires of disillusion

My magnificent faith
now carries insurance
I keep it locked in the trunk
with the spare and the jack

Optimism replaced
by its flip side: pragmatism

I undersell the possible
avoid side trips
stay on the main highway
even though it seems to go nowhere

I long for a backroad excursion
to pop the trunk
just long enough
to let my latent faith escape

or at least
catch some fresh air.

Amplitude – Shoulder – Lark

Every inhalation contains amplitude.

While a sine wave is symmetrical,
life's timing of oscillations
between peak and trough
is asymmetrical, so
remains ambiguous.

Regardless,
a wave stagnant at crest
will be no wave at all,
will become a flat line
implying death ⋯ yet

we seem intent on finding
one high after another,
shunning the low points,
fearful of the valley's shadow.

We hike to the peak,
refuse to come down,
scramble frantic
along the apex ridge,
holding to the harsh alpine light.

We cannot bear to shoulder
what might await us
in the trough,
so we push the frequency,
we tighten the wave form
into a high-pitched cry
of *Carpe diem*!

How do we cease our seizing?

What is the Latin translation
of *Receive the day?*

*Sume diem.*

How do our nervous hearts
receive with equivalent significance
the lark's morning revelries,
the nightingale's midnight melodies?

A truer abundance
will surely fill us
when we seek
this equilibrium.

*Sume diem.*

Cedar – Habitat – Sabbatical

If I could take a sabbatical,
a leave with pay for rejuvenation,

I would seek out a wild habitat
for my too tamed mind,
a place with elevation, a wide view,
a few cedar and juniper trees,
an aspen grove on a high slope.

A place where sunlight plays
on granite and the emerald skin of lakes.

A place where I can breathe thinner air,
bathe in alpine coolness,
and remember from where I came,

and remember my own name,

and remember the nature
of the golden ratio,
and the shape of change.

Saunter – Cast – Headway

The slow road
is the one less traveled.

Speed, the pandemic addiction.

What is cast away
as dross from the mill
of making incessant headway?

The treasures of a saunter
on a pilgrimage of meaning.

Feel of earth on the sole.
Scent of new rain on grass.
Song of autumn's last cricket.

Feel of Earth on the soul.

Irrepressible – Fickle – Pull

I decide to stop writing.

I decide to resist
this irrepressible pull

to anchor
each impressionable
moment
to some rocky shoal
of conviction

to marry
my fickle heart
to my flighty mind

as if fickle combined
with flighty
might ignite
an alchemical
combustion
resulting in wisdom

I decide to stop writing

trying to make concrete
what is irrefutably
abstract, pliable,
undefinable.

I decide to stop.

Reverse – Crevice – Multifaceted

The past
is not a place
on a map
we visited last week,
last year,
three decades ago.

There is no traversed road.
No option to reverse course,
to go back and fetch
our favorite, well-worn hat
left behind at that diner
with the chrome and red vinyl.

The past
is a crystalline matrix
so multifaceted
a single event is prismatic
reflecting a full spectrum.

The angle of observance
changes the recollected
nature of an occurrence.

The mind holds the past
as a jigsaw puzzle undone.

Pieces strewn willy-nilly
as if by a williwaw
across the incongruous
topography of thought.

Many fall into crevices
too deep to be retrieved.

The past is not what we believed.
It is encrypted mystery.

## Oleander – Chimera – Performance

I am walking a hedge
maze of oleander, red
as the flaming exhale
of an ancient chimera

I walk on broken
roof tiles, red
as a late lingering sun

Six incandescent dragon
flies flit about my head
as escorts

There is a river
of marigolds
I pass through barefoot
staining my soles
the color of holy robes

In this performance
art of living
knowing the steps
is of no consequence

the music always unfamiliar
the movement impromptu

When I step out of these robes

I will become a dragon
flying with chimera's breath

Raven – Frontispiece – Scrawl

In the frontispiece of the volume,
a delicate pen and ink print,
a raven sits in a barren tree
staring intently at the reader
as if to screech,

Beware!

The handwritten scrawl
beneath his beak,
barely legible reads,

Know Thyself.

That ancient Greek maxim
inscribed in the forecourt
of the Temple of Apollo at Delphi.

Raven, in Tlingit mythology,
is a transformative figure
and, like Coyote in the
Southwest, a trickster.

Beware!

Know Thyself!

I think of you, in your late years,
though you will never have them now,
turning these dog-eared pages
seeking to reach a cryptic wisdom
by delving deep
into this medieval poetry.

Be aware.

Know Thyself.

## Sitting – Mentor – Conscious

Silence,
mentor me.

Help me hold
my seat.

Sitting here,

hearing
internal turmoil turn
itself inside-out.

Listening
without
hooking in.

Silence,
mentor me.

Bring me into
conscious presence.

Leave me free,
at peace.

Silence,
mentor me.

## Excavate – Recumbent – Artifact

The task at hand,
to excavate meaning
from the gifts and dross
of chaotic coincidence.

Each uncovered artifact
dusted off cautiously,
observed, turned, catalogued.

What stretch across the tension
pulls us apart, lays bare
our fragile ribs,
reveals our tender cardiology?

As we dig, recumbent
on the sedimentary deposits,
what petroglyphs appear,
expose their frozen hunts
to refresh our bone-held memory?

Swoon – Engineer – Matrilineal

I don't swoon
over imaginary numbers.

Differential equations
create no ecstatic buzz
of pleasure in my brain.

I do find String Theory,
and astrophysics fascinating.

I am super fast with calculus
but only on my back molars.

I haven't encountered
a 2 molar solution
since tenth grade.

I do enjoy order.

Matrilineal genetic patterns,
my mom's dad being an engineer,
passed down to give me
a fastidious set theory
whenever I pack a suitcase.

I swoon
over pragmatic
organization.

## Half-hearted – Gusto – Habit

To pump the blood
with pulmonary gusto
through artery and vein
and all the capillaries,
takes all four chambers
of the valiant muscle.

The habit of life
dependent on routine.

Still, daily patterns
erode the fervor
of the doing,

leaving us half-hearted
in habitual spin.

How do we imbue
enthusiasm
back in,

begin anew?

## Scripture – Tanager – Lifeboat

Scripture
as distillation
of accumulated wisdom.

Scripture
as incandescent stones
laid painstakingly
along a path to clarity.

Scripture
as lifeboat
when the ship goes under,
when the gale blinds sight,
and thunder deafens the mind.

Scripture
as scarlet tanager
singing in the tree
of reconnection,

lauding praise
for all life-forms.

Scripture
as a fine line of guidance
to transmute anger to love,
vengeance to forgiveness,
despair to hope.

Scripture
as quiet mind
alight with compassion.

## Halting – Dark Horse – Signify

The problem with trauma,
barring the obvious,
is the sublingual
longevity of it,

the bitter lingering aftertaste,
the lack of closure cultivating
a persistent foreboding.

Multiple traumatic incidents
triggering Chicken Little
again and again.

When I give the track record
of the past the right to signify
the track record of the future,

I expect the sky to fall.

I falter, consternate.

This halting cadence
is no way to run the race.

Today, I forfeit
my hardwired habit
of fortune-telling.

Today, I am the dark horse.

# Album Three

*The Nature of Change*

## Osprey – Sapphire – Canopy

Lake Alpine licks granite
islands sparingly tipped
with bristlecone pine.

Overhead, an osprey
with wind under her weight,
canopy of soft white cloud
over her singing shape,
scans the fish-rich water.

Rainbow trout glisten
beneath sapphire surface,
evading fishermen's lures,
the osprey's hunger.

My lime kayak
floats over the glint,
her hull a safe respite
for periwinkle damselflies.

The osprey dives,
a strategic hit,
alights with her catch
in knife-sharp talons.

Retake – Tender – Duet

This late light, on the cusp of winter

This low sun throws amber on bare trees,
hazes over distance in greying pinks

Obscures the west in blinding glare

This late light haunts
with ghosts of bygone years

As I drive south along fallow fields
of plowed under raw sienna

This late light haunts

In this early December, I burst

with a tender yearning to relive
spring, summer, fall,

retake all with greater abandon

As the sun's orb skirts mountain ridges,
the range of light shortens, shadows grow

I feel the silent urgency of unsprung green,
of still dormant seed in frigid soil

Two Swainson's hawks sweep the mauve sky,
a duet of wings and talons
gracing the day's end with avian blessing.

If I could hold the sun suspended,
keep her molten globe in my upturned palm,

as homage,

I would gladly burn.

## Nimble – Frenetic – Trimming

Walking along the creek trail,
Silence turns to rushing water,
but the creek is low, almost stagnant.

This quick river over stone song
is the collective chatter of a thousand
starlings, scattered in the branches
of a massive Valley Oak.

Their grey-black shapes trim
the heritage tree like
ornithological ornaments.

Their cacophonous chorus ceases,
instantaneously to a uniform quiet,
just prior to their lifting,
en masse, a black cloud
in nimble formation,
flitting, frenetic, polka
dotting the December blue sky
with triangles of synchronized wings.

An Escher etching.

I marvel, agape,
as I stare straight up
into the flock's mosaic
murmuration.

## Waterfall – Quartz – Slick

I approach the distant roar of the waterfall,
its white-water cascade not yet visible.

A perfectly aligned vein of quartz,
in relief from the alluvial due to eons
of unrelenting spring runoff,
creates a sparkling white highway.

I hike along the two-foot wide dry ridge
running through the lichen-slick flats,
straight as an arrow pointing the way
to the base of Bassi Falls,

where the origin of this vein's slow,
time-worn upward revelation pounds down
thunderous over rounded granite rocks
with calamitous force and sound.

Tymbal – Externalism – Taffeta

to possess a shrilling organ
as does a cicada
to sing with sinew
ceaselessly

to resonate
a plaintive rustling
of taffeta
over tile
a swish
of wishes

as one
expressing
externalism
in fashionable
whimsy

the other
a vibrating
tymbal
of instinct

a woman
in the ballroom

a cicada
in the garden

## Sensitize – Apothecary – Porous

A copper mortar and pestle,
origin Holland, as is my own,
rests on the top shelf of the bookcase,
gleaming with Vermeer light.

Objects hold subjective meaning
sensitize the observer
to personal and cultural archeology.

Objects also hold objective meaning,
a truth pooled within the object itself,
as a porous membrane absorbs
the essential substance of events.

Microscopic remnants of belladonna
embedded in a physical history.
What was ground down
within this copper vessel
remains as ghost halo.

The workings of an apothecary.
The confidence in a cure.

Revisit – Monologue – Finesse

The actress steps out
from the curtained wings,
moves stage left, deftly
with the ease of decades of plays,
finding her light, center stage
before the darkened house
with its hushed anticipation,
the heat of the Fresnels,
through bastard amber gels,
illuminating her angled features.

She reaches far beyond
the audience she cannot see,
launches into the monologue,
not a trace of the monotony
of show after show,
week after week.
Each word delivered here
is fresh, the finesse
of gestures more natural
than her own will be,
later at the after-party,
when she will feel alien
in her skin, no character
to find herself in.

After the theater is cold,
all chairs empty, except
for the ghosts of the years,
she will revisit the stage,
walk the scuffed boards,
replay her performance
in her mind, refine,
file the minor rough edges
to an ever more immaculate
chance at perfection.

## Sepia – Narrow – Homograph

Sepia tones invoke
times past, hold histories
of the strong arms of loggers,
pioneers, prospectors,
bustled ladies
in wide-brimmed hats,
laden horses loaded up
on muddy main streets.

In narrow framed daguerrotypes,
life looks serious without its colors.

Early films clicking on metal reels
compress real life into jolts and jerks,
infuse movement with a humor
forlorn faces refuse to evoke.

What is real is never fully
transferable to translucent film.

The photographer never content
with the content of his camera.

The project never projects
the life it tries to capture.
The subject is always subject
to subjective perception.

When we have wound
the documentary
onto the metal reel,

the real wound
stops bleeding,
but the tear
can still tear
at the heart.

Such is the nature
of the homograph.

Such is the gift
of the film,
or the photograph.

Bumblebee – Skin – Flight

The musical piece, *Flight of the Bumblebee*,
by Rimsky-Korsakov, renders the zigzag,
rag-tag, rollercoaster, dizzy dart, flower flirting
flight of the bulbous bee in the frenetic ascending,
descending rapid fire scale in the key of C.

The bumblebee is a buzz pollinator.
He clings to the skin of a blackberry blossom.
Hanging upside down, he activates his flight muscles,
buzzing to shake loose the yellow pollen
inside the bloom's tube onto his vibrating belly,
from where he collects the golden sticky substance
onto his hind legs to carry it safely back
to nourish the hive.

His buzz pollination
resonates at Concert Pitch,
a frequency of 440 Hz,
the note A above middle C,
the standard reference
used to tune an orchestra
internationally.

## Precipitate – Chartreuse – Wallflower

The season proclaims it,
year after year,
loss precipitates renewal.

This restive wind combing
through chartreuse fields.

This gnarled almond blossoming
in ghost snow adornment.

This great horned owl nest
filled with fluff and chick hunger.

Another romping painted egg hunt,
munching walnuts at Winter Creek Ranch,
where Sam and Caroline coax
a joyous, wacky ambience
that plucks wallflowers
off their demure haunts.

I no longer count anniversaries
of disappointment. I am too busy
collecting the pollen of friendship.

## Humpback – Rush – Ideal

Out there, just beyond the wave break,
I see them, three Humpback whales.
In placid waters with minimal surf,
their massive girth and agile backs curve up
out of the slick blue in late afternoon sun.

My eyes stay glued to their every movement,
their skyward salutes of tail flukes.
My heart is a trapeze artist in mid-flight.
I am mesmerized, enchanted, gleeful.

I stand still, outside of time,
watching like a child at the circus,
until they are gone, deep sea seeking.

I call a friend who owns kayaks,
get his voicemail, leave a message,
wait for a return call, grow antsy. Nothing.

Next day, in the wet grey of early morning,
My friend arrives unannounced at the door.
We strap his two-person kayak to the roof rack,
drive to the marina, launch the purple sit-a-top.
Paddle out into a thick, obscuring fog.

Not ideal weather for sea going, or for seeing,
but it is completely calm, not even a slight breeze.

White mist sky meets mercurial sea, no sign of horizon.
A still weak sun illuminates a borderless universe.

We will not seek them out, we'll just be present and wait.

Then we hear it, very close to our meager boat,
an unmistakable sound, the loud rush of air expelled
from the blowhole of a 40 ton marine mammal.
The potent odor of methane accosts our nostrils.

The black shape of the behemoth rises like an island.
A posy of hungry seals appears out of nowhere.
Hundreds of slick brown bodies head straight for us,
raucous honks of disapproval at our sitting in their diner,
though, technically, the Humpback owns the place outright.

We see him resurface, his massive shining back arching.
He is not alone. A second whale becomes a submarine
to starboard, dives down, is submerged directly below us.

Pelicans arrive, dive reckless into the fray.
Then a sound like a thousand strips of raw bacon
thrown into a well-oiled skillet, just off our bow.

The sea boils with a fevered hissing,
as thousands of silver mackerel shoot up
in a frenzied attempt at escape into air.

There is only one explanation, and it arrives quickly,
giant jaws agape, scooping up a cauldron of doomed fish.

The Humpback's head rises five feet out of the sea,
the completion of its bubble net feeding,
straining water through baleen, swallowing its meal.

He is a mere fifteen feet from our hushed wows.
We ought to feel fear, but experience only rapture,
a sacred encounter captured by our reverent souls.

## Whalebone – Whitecap – Whacked-Out

On the sun streaked concrete
of the Marine Mammal Center
lies a bleached whalebone
the size of an outrigger.

This half of a Humpback jawbone
puts me up close and personal
with the real hazard of my own
recent proximity to a feeding whale.

I could easily have been thrown
from the slender kayak, with a broken
collar bone from a mere tap
of tail fluke or flap of a flipper.

I could easily have been tossed
like a breadcrumb into the sea,
unable to swim, shark bait,
miracle becoming cruel fate.

My lucky to be alive feet
stand between the jawbone
and the knee high vertebrae
of the ancient whale, juxtaposed
to expose my vulnerable size.

Favorite – Unbounded – Crushing

North inner cove of Monterey Bay
Mediterranean overlay
in pastel colors painted
on the Capitola Venetian Hotel
across watery blue haze

Southern stretch
of Rio del Mar Beach
favorite hideaway
expanse of fawn sand
traversed in early morning

Dolphins curve along
light-embraced waves,
as they feed on sardines

Black neoprene
makes a seal of me
gliding on white foam
after the crash
of crushing brine,
surging seawater
carries me on my
Morey boogie board
towards sunlit shore

Unbounded joy

## Layer – Stand – Rational

Science claims to be a rational,
intelligent act of exposing
reality, layer by layer.

Yet, as the objects
and phenomena exposed
are clinically observed,
the layers deepen,
and reality proves
to be a spiraling mystery.

To stand before the expanding
universe of the unknown,
to witness the diffusion
of macro and micro horizons
to infinity,
is to acknowledge
that science
is a mystical pilgrimage,
an act of faith
in the potential
for understanding.

## Rocketry – Diffraction – Kidnap

In the science of rocketry,
you calculate the thrust
required to force your projectile,
by means of fiery combustion,
beyond the counter pull of gravity
and the drag of atmosphere.

This means that the forces
pushing the object in one direction
are greater than the forces
pulling it in the opposite direction.

Moving a divorced woman over fifty
from a hometown of thirty years
takes a monumental thrust
of unbalanced force.

All of my prior launch attempts,
weekend trips to the coast,
were merely soul soothing detours,
miscalculations of true trajectory.

Ultimately, the required thrust
was to kidnap myself blindfolded,
or be kidnapped by love,
and carry myself into the precarious,

despite, and in defiance of the gravity
of that five-story parking garage roof
from which you took your final
free fall between worlds.

To eject myself from the cocooned
discomfort of a minimal security,
and the painful recollections of betrayal
into the diffraction of desert light,
by impetus of an undefined life,

my own free fall between worlds.

# Album Four

*Southwest Renewal*

## Meltdown – Reckless – Harebrained

Let me begin
with the basic premise
that grasping the zebra's mane
on this merciless merry-go-round
is a harebrained operation
requiring untold courage,
a wily intrepid desire
to see it through
no matter what!

Let me begin
at the point of meltdown
and work backwards
from there
to the reckless
chase of sperm
toward egg,
the against all odds zygote,
the preposterous
propagation of the embryo,

Let me begin.

## West – Lackluster – Convert

We came west
to convert a lackluster life
to the excitement of barren buttes,
bawdy barrooms, brazen cactus blooms.

We came west
to overt topographies,
obtuse angles of open sky,
the aching dissonant
harmonies of coyotes.

We came west
to avert family strife,
economic stagnation,
religious constriction,
a too close horizon.

We came west
to a perverted promise of gold,
to escape from the cold,
to obtain a piece of hardscrabble,
dry, stubborn but owned land.

We came west
to assert our personal freedom,
our disdain for restrictions,
our counterculture convictions.

The only west
left to us now
is the abstract expanse
of the Pacific,
the Eden call of Hawaii,
the mysteries of the Orient.

We go east
to convert
the harassment
of too much,
and the weight
of never enough

into quiet mind.

## Hilltop – Supposed – Notice

You could say,
I should have taken notice
of time passing,
one loaded down
freight car after another,
a long line humming north,
four engines in the front,
two in the rear, pushing
a whole lot of dead weight,
graffiti laden, creaking.

You could say,
how did I miss
the increasing strain
of metal to rail,
as engines wailed
up one hilltop after another,
under brilliant constellations,
under hellish sun glare?

Was I supposed to be aware
of my own age accumulating,
my slow amassing of years?

Sure, I heard the gears
churning away,
felt the deep exhaustion
of self-knowledge

ache to the bone.

But on the inside,
that small, innocent
faith I maintain
flares, resonates.

Can you tell me,
where to find
an abandoned rail yard
where I can decouple the bulk
of these moaning boxcars,
leave their disheveled
hulks on a side track,

donate their shade making
shelters in an expanse
of rarely traversed desert?

I need to feel that release,
pare down to a single engine,
travel what remains of the trek
with only the essentials,
the core concepts,
the vital memories,
the basic befuddlements
of awe.

## Sandstone – Discontented – Southwest

I have a nagging inclination,
an intuitive hunch,
a near physical itch,
to see if being in
the Southwest will vitalize
my discontented spirit.

Social churches never seem to speak
the unique language of my soul,
while wilderness speaks it fluently.

Living here, wilderness is hours away,
a long trek on treacherous highways.

In the desert, light itself is wilderness,
the expanse of view invites rapture.

You can witness the approach of rain
from eighty miles away, sweeping
towards you as a grey curtain.

Wherever that curtain falls,
the potent scent of piñon and sage
arrest the olfactory sense.

That is a church I could attend,
at least for a time, to provide my life
with a horizon to breathe out into.

Do I have the courage and fortitude
to make the leap, to convert to a church
with only the stained glass windows of sunrise?

## Motherland – Flank – Pungent

It was only a week-long vacation,
in late July, during which it rained,
not just afternoons, but non-stop,
making me wonder if I was in Portland,
rather than Santa Fe, in the high desert.

It was only a week-long trial
to ascertain whether this high plateau
at the flank of the Rockies,
here called the Sangre de Cristos,
the Blood of Christ mountains,
had potential to be my true
motherland, my new home turf.

It was only a week-long investigation
on foot, as the rental car made my back
scream in pain, and the rental company
refused to let me to trade the F Torture,
as I came to call it, for another model.

It was only a week-long sojourn
to smell the sweetness of piñon
to breathe in the aroma of wet cedar
and pungent juniper in the monsoon,
to see if my bones could love this soil.

It was only a week-long blur
of ponderosa pine and aspen
on hiking trails in the forest
only a few miles from the Plaza,
where native men and women
sat at the Palace of the Governors,
the oldest continuously occupied
public building in the United States,
selling their silver and turquoise
on blankets under the portico.

What could I know of this city's soul?

## Haphazard – Quota – Capitulate

Meeting you on the penultimate
day of my first investigative trip,
when I questioned if these vistas
might not be mine after all.

Leaving only to discover
our connection growing stronger,
a bond of genuine friendship
urging me to return again.

Your offer to help me move,
a lifeline to a new future
I'd be a fool to refuse.

Do we each have a quota of luck,
an inheritance of good fortune,
a nest egg of miraculous intervention?

If so, I'm grateful mine
were not yet used up.

Are all the haphazard interactions,
circumstances, quirks of coincidence
more synchronous than random?

What happens when we capitulate
to fate, as I believe we did?

A coherence of conditions
leading to the superb
enigma of here.

## Vocation – Hike – Arid

I came to the high desert to hike,
to have access to wildness
right outside my backdoor.

Living here, I walk, not drive,
to the nearest designated
wilderness area, where paw prints
of mountain lions form intaglio
in the half-dried mud, or fresh snow.

In twenty minutes, I can drive
up into the National Forest,
where Ponderosa pine and aspen
stand taller than their average height.

I stand taller here as well.
My vocation arguably
to walk in natural beauty,
and write the language of wonder,
the argot of poets.

This land is arid yet green
with juniper and piñon.
These untethered views unsettle
my psyche with their bold expanse,
yet the rattling frees me.

This is a land of ristras,
chamiso, arroyos, mesas,
pueblos, katchinas,
Anasazi ruins, and casinos.

I do not yet speak its vigorous
vernacular, but daily
I am tutored by coyotes,
jackrabbits, and green chili peppers.

## Naturalist – Saturate – Heliocentric

It is the undulating,
interwoven web
of light reflections
that holds me
transfixed

keeps me swimming
back and forth
gliding along
through an element
thicker than air,
more luminous,

a naturalist
in this turquoise
realm of buoyancy

exploiting
my heliocentric
desire
to subsume

this translucence

saturate my senses
with its ebullience.

## Granulate – Slough – Evidence

This terrain is banded evidence
of a prehistoric eruption,
a super volcano's glory day,
blowing the crown off
a mountain the size of Rainier.

Here among the shadowboxed
canyons, bastard amber sandstone
is mixed with ashen, porous igneous,
an eons worn granulate
sloughed off over millennia.

Globules of pumice
scattered over the alluvial
like rune stones thrown,
as divination of doom.

Here there is more room
than the eye can capture
or the brain can assimilate,
a surreal scenery, untouchable
by common comprehension.

## Scenery – Expansive – Well-being

Exactly a year ago today,
a 26-foot U-Haul truck pulls
into my unpaved driveway.

After a solid month of letting go
of clothes, chairs, tables, dishes,
pans, lamps, hammocks, hats, shoes,
my beloved boogie board, kayak,
eight bookcases and their contents;
after four massive yard sales
and daily *free* signs on the sidewalk,

I have a room full of packed boxes,
dressers, furniture, a Nordic Track,
and three burly men taking them
all away, stacking what remains
of my belongings into a jigsaw
puzzle of organized chaos
in the cavernous interior of the truck.

On the other end of the journey,
this puzzle will be taken apart,
piece by piece, each item placed,
expectant of stability, into an
expansive landscape of hope

that in a state with scenery unbound,
a new well-being might, slowly
and surely, find me, as rain slips down
into dry arroyos, and the past slips away

into the mythic.

## Indian Summer – Fetish – Cliffhanger

The Zuni carve stone fetishes.
The *Wemawe* are animal spirits,
healers, keepers of the sacred.

This one is a black rabbit,
an inch tall, sitting on haunches,
but a towering fertile power.
Carved out of jet with inlaid
turquoise eyes, a gift for my
mother, whose eyes are failing.

The Hopi make kachina dolls
carved from cottonwood roots.
The *Katsintithu* are spirit guides,
immortal beings, messengers.

We bring them home.

    Corn Dancer
    Koshare Clown
    Crow Mother
    Grandmother
    Sun-faced Dancer
    White Chin
    Mountain Lion
    Great Horned Owl

We also invite three fetishes.

Cottontail Rabbit
White Bear
Prairie Dog

Great Spirit obeys their prayers.
Ours are answered.

Indian summer lingers sultry,
a last bastion of unbridled light.

Finally, our cliffhangers resolve.
We don't just reside here.
We fully arrive.

Infiltrate – Beget – Upward

In the sign language
of the body
written in sinew

your touch infiltrates
my defenses
like a regimen
of cautious gardeners
bulbs in hand
ready to plant
what love will beget.

Dark soil will enable
this thrusting upward
across strata of loss

towards a new trust.

## About the Author

Eve West Bessier is an award-winning writer. Her work is widely published in journals and anthologies. Eve is Poet Laureate of Silver City, New Mexico (2019-2021). She is also a Poet Laureate Emerita of Davis, California (2012-2014). Eve was born in the Netherlands. She and her mom immigrated to San Francisco when Eve was seven. She holds a Bachelor of Arts in English and Creative Writing from San Francisco State University, and a Master of Education from the University of California, Davis. Eve is a social scientist and educator. She is a studio musician, jazz vocalist, voice coach, and life coach. She performs her unique blend of vocal jazz and original poetry at conferences, house concerts, art galleries, and other venues. You can hear her recordings and watch her videos on her website.

www.jazzpoetve.com

www.ingramcontent.com/pod-product-compliance
Lightning Source LLC
Chambersburg PA
CBHW051655040426
42446CB00009B/1155